The Novello Youth Chorals

Music of the World

For SATB Choir With Piano Accompaniment

Arranged by Jeremy Jackman

Published by:
Novello Publishing Limited
8/9 Frith Street, London W1D 3JB, England.

Exclusive distributors:
Music Sales Limited
Distribution Centre, Newmarket Road, Bury St Edmunds, Suffolk IP33 3YB.

Music Sales Pty Limited
120 Rothschild Avenue, Rosebery, NSW 2018, Australia.

Order No. NOV200223
ISBN 1-84449-003-3
This collection © Copyright 2003 Novello & Company Limited.

Music engraved by Andrew Shiels.
Compiled by Jo Dachey.
Printed in the United Kingdom.

www.musicsales.com

Novello Publishing Limited
London / New York / Paris / Sydney / Copenhagen / Berlin / Madrid / Tokyo

Notes

Ai, Dunaii Moy
(Ah, My Dunaii)
from Russia

If you think you have heard this melody before – you have! It appears in Tchaikovsky's *1812 Overture*. The text, with so many long words and so much repetition, does little more than set a scene. I have provided an alternative English text for those who really feel the Russian is beyond them, but the piece will sound more authentic in the original language.

Pronunciation guide:

u = *"oo"* as in *"loot"*

kh = *"ch"* as in Scottish *"loch"*

ai = *"aye"* as in *"Aye, aye, Captain!"*

ü = German *"ü"*, or the French *"u"*, as in *"tu"*

zh = *"j"* as in French *"je"*

moy = rhymes with English *"toy"*

La Cucaracha
(The Cockroach)
from Mexico

This exhilarating song conjures up images of fiesta, so it is a 'party-piece' in more senses than one. You will arrive at the right sound instantly if you remember that Spanish vowels are as bright as the South American sun! The text is a collection of wide-ranging nonsense, mixed up with a bit of Mexican history. Keep it bright!

Pronunciation guide:

j = *"ch"* as in Scottish *"loch"*

ll = *"ly"* as in *"polio"*

x = *h*

qu = *k*

The letters "b" and "v" are virtually interchangeable and sound like a cross between the two!

Translation:

Verse 1.   All the girls have in their eyes two stars,
But Mexican girls certainly are more beautiful.

Verse 2.	Girls are of gold, ladies are of silver,
	Widows are of copper, old women are of tin-plate.

Verse 3.	One thing makes me laugh, Pancho Villa without his shirt,
	Now the followers of Carranzo go away because the (Pancho) Villa
	supporters are coming.

Chorus.	*The cockroach doesn't want to go anywhere,*
	Because he hasn't any . . . because he lacks . . . money to spend.

Lomir Sich Iberbetn
(Let Us Be Lovers Again)
Yiddish

This is a Yiddish love song, with typical characteristics in the melody which will be recognised by anyone who has practised harmonic minor scales on their instruments! The language is not difficult to pronounce, being similar to German in some respects. (Yiddish "borrows" from many different sources of which the main one is German.) Thus, "ch" is pronounced as in Scottish *"loch"*, and "z" is *"ts"*. However "i" is longer than German; more like *"ee"* in English.

Pronunciation guide: lo-mir = *"mir"* to rhyme with *"deer"*
sich i - ber - be - tn = *zeech ee - ber - bay - tn*
c'h'ob = *"ch"* as in Scottish *"loch"*
shteistu = *shtay-stoo*
tir = *tayr*
kum = *kim*
arein = *aryn* (rhymes with *"fine"*)
zu = *zi*

Translation:

Verse 1.	Lomir sich iberbetn,	*Let us be lovers again,*
	Hob af mir rachmones,	*Have pity on me,*
	C'h'ob dir lib sakones.	*You are the love of my life.*

Verse 2.	Vos shteistu far der tir?	*Why do you stand outside the door?*
	Kum arein zu mir.	*Come in to me.*

Verse 3.	Loz di mamen vissn.	*Let your mother know.*
	Fùn libe genissn.	*Let us enjoy love.*

Manthi'ki
(Spirit Song)
from Zimbabwe

In the Ndau tradition (Zimbabwe), healing is performed by a Diviner who absorbs a spirit for the purpose. This is the people's song: the spirit's work is done, and with their singing they persuade it to depart. The text likens the spirit to a bird, thus:

> Nya - m'nje - nje w'e - nda ku - mba kwa - ke,
> *The bird flies homeward,*
>
> Shi - li - ma - ji - we ma - ji,
> *Bird of the ocean,*
>
> Shi - li mb'lu - ka.
> *Now fly away.*

At the cry of "Wensia", the spirit departs. The words are pronounced exactly as one would expect; the letter "j" as in the English word *"jam"* and the final "-ia" in "Wensia" is very close together as in *"piano"*.

The only aspect of this arrangement that is likely to produce any difficulty at all is the junction between bars 20 & 21. This is made easier when we remember that the end of bar 20 $\left[\begin{array}{c}\text{♫} \text{♪}\\ \text{wo ye.}\end{array}\right]$ and the beginning of bar 21 $\left[\begin{array}{c}\text{♪ ♫ ♩}\\ \text{Shi - li - ma}\end{array}\right]$ are sung within the same ♩. time.

The optional descant which occurs in two short places need only be sung by a few voices (or even one voice!), but it is preferable to include these notes.

Pescator Dell'Onda
(Fisherman From The Waves)
from Italy

This fishy tale may well be Sicilian in origin. If you have never sung in Italian before you may find the words of the chorus tongue-twisting at first, but Italian is such a delicious language to pronounce that with practice the words will trip off the tongue. *Fédéri* would appear to be the sailor's name; it has overtones of loyalty and trust ("fede" in Italian means "faith").

If desired, the effect at the opening can be cumulative, with one or a few voices entering at ① and more added successively at ② and ③, so that by bar 10, all are singing.

Pronunciation: The words are pronounced exactly as one might expect. To clear up any doubt, the "s" in "cosa" (v.3) is pronounced like an English *"z"*, otherwise all "s" sounds are as in English *"sun"*.

"Ch" = *"k"* as is the letter "c" before the letter "a".

> e.g.   "pescator" = *"pesskator"*

Before the letter "e" and "i", "c" = *"ch"*.

> e.g.   "cento" = *"chento"*
>
> "bacin" = *"bachin"*

Others to watch out for:

> "Qu" = *"kw"*
>
> "Gh" = hard *"g"* as in English *"gap"*

Translation:

Verse 1.   O fisherman from the waves, *O Fédéri!*
Come and fish here,
With your beautiful boat,
She goes like a beauty,
Fédéri, lin, la!

Verse 2.   Come and fish for my ring, *O Fédéri!*
Which fell into the sea.

Verse 3.   The ring is already fished out, *O Fédéri!*
What are you going to give me?

Verse 4.   I'll give you a hundred scudi, *O Fédéri!*
To enrich (lit. "to embroider") your purse.

Verse 5.   He doesn't want a hundred scudi, *O Fédéri!*
Nor a fat wallet.

Verse 6.   He wants a loving kiss, *your Fédéri!*
Which he will pay for.

Acknowledgements
The author would like to thank:
Ruth Schneider for her help with the translation of *Lomir Sich Iberbetn*, Daniela Mo and Louisa and Guido Maestranzi for their help with *Pescator Dell'Onda*, Natalia Shoutova for her help with the text in *Ai, Dunaii Moy* and Paco and Isabel Sudea for their help with *La Cucaracha*.

Ai, Dunaii Moy
(Ah, My Dunaii)

from Russia

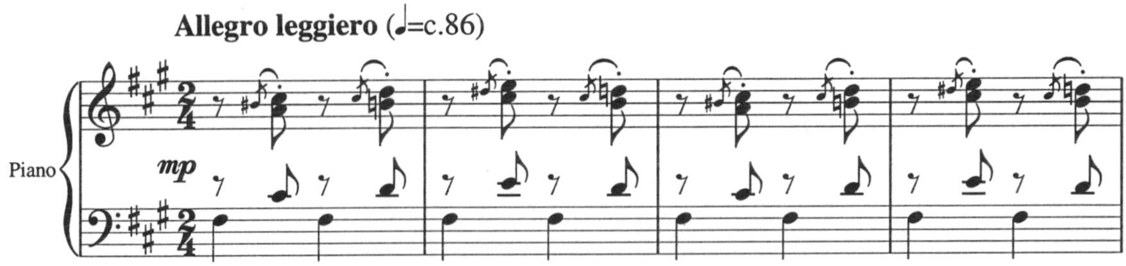

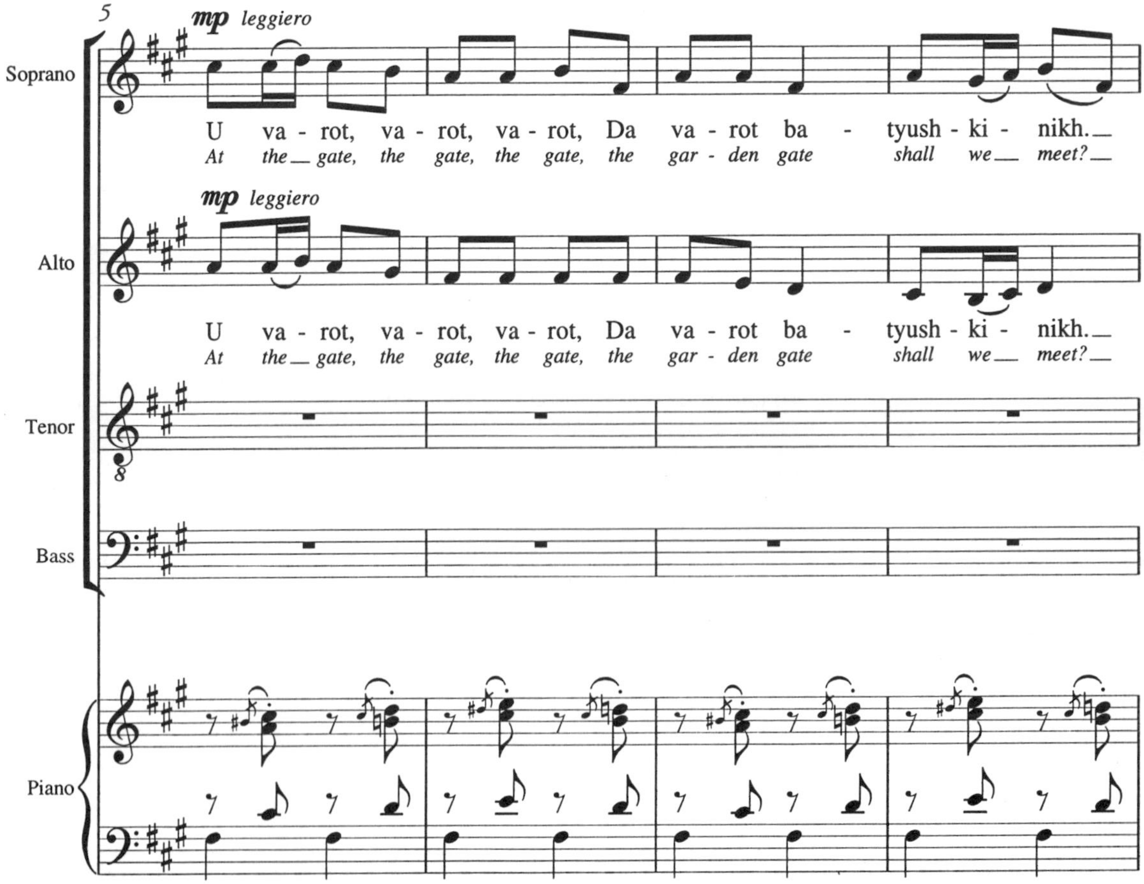

Ai, Du - naii moy Du naii,— Ai, ve - syo - lyi Du - naii.—
Ah, Du - naii, my Du - naii,— Ah, dear - est dear Du - naii.—

Ah,_____ Ah,_____

Ah,_____ Ah,_____

Ah,_____ Ah,_____

Oo_____

Oo_____

Ra - zü - gra - lí - sya ria - bya - ta, Ras - po - te_____ shi - lis.___
If we see the child - ren__ play - ing, They won't hear_____ me say - ing.

(*mp*)

17
mf
mp
Ai, Du - naii moy Du - naii, Ai, ve - syo - lyi Du - naii.
Ah, Du - naii my Du - naii, Ah, dear - est dear Du - naii.
Ai, Du - naii moy Du - naii, Ai, ve - syo - lyi Du - naii.
Ah, Du - naii my Du - naii, Ah, dear - est dear Du - naii.
Ai, Du - naii moy Du - naii, Ai, ve - syo - lyi Du - naii.
Ah, Du - naii my Du - naii, Ah, dear - est dear Du - naii.
Ai, Du - naii moy Du - naii, Ai, Du - naii.
Ah, Du - naii my Du - naii, Ah, Du - naii.
21
mp

25
mf leggiero
Tenor
U va - rot, va - rot, va - rot, Da va - rot ba - tyush - ki - nikh.
At the gate, the gate, the gate, the gar - den gate shall we meet?
mf leggiero
Bass
U va - rot, va - rot, va - rot, Da va - rot ba - tyush - ki - nikh.
At the gate, the gate, the gate, the gar - den gate shall we meet?
Piano
29
mf legato
Ai, Du - naii moy Du - naii, Ai, ve - syo - lyi Du - naii.
Ah, Du - naii, my Du - naii, Ah, dear - est dear Du - naii.
mf legato
Ah, Ah,
mf legato
Ah, Ah,
mf legato
Ah, Ah,

33
leggiero
Ra - zü - gra - lí - sya ria - bya - ta,
If we see the child - ren play - ing,
Ras - po - te shi - lis
They won't hear me say - ing,
37
rit.
Ai, Du - naii moy Du - naii, Ai, ve - syo - lyi Du - naii.
Ah, Du - naii, my Du - naii, Ah, dear - est dear Du - naii.
rit.
Ai, ve - syo - lyi Du - naii.
Ah, dear - est dear Du - naii.
rit.
Ai, ve - syo - lyi Du - naii.
Ah, dear - est dear Du - naii.
rit.
Ai, Du - naii.
Ah, Du - naii.
rit.

41
a tempo
a tempo
a tempo
a tempo
mf leggiero
Od - no - mu - to mo - lod - tsu khu - do mo - zhed tsya.
Yet I know one poor fel - low, Vic - tim of sad fate.
a tempo
45
mp legato
Ah, ah ah, ah
mf legato
Ai, Du - naii moy Du - naii, Ai, ve - syo - lyi Du - naii.
Ah, Du - naii my Du - naii, Ah, dear - est dear Du - naii.
mf legato
Du - naii, moy Du - naii, ve - syo - lyi Du - naii.
Du - naii, my Du - naii, dear - est dear Du - naii.
mp legato
Ah, ah,

mf leggiero
Nez - da - ro - vit - sya
Love is no trea - sure,
mf leggiero
Khu - do mo - zhed tsya
Life is no plea - sure,
mf leggiero
Khu - do mo - zhed tsya Nez da - ro - vit - sya.
Life is no plea - sure, Love is no trea - sure,
53
mp legato
Ah, ah, Du - naii.
Ah, ah, Du - naii.
mp legato
Ai, Du - naii moy, Du - naii, Ai, ves - yo - lyi Du - naii.
Ah, Du - naii my, Du - naii, Ah, dear - est dear Du - naii.
mp legato
Ah, Ah, Du - naii.
mp legato
Ah, Ah, Du - naii.

U va - rot, va - rot, va - rot, Da va - rot ba - tyush - ki - nikh.
At the __ gate, the gate, the gate, the gar - den gate shall we __ meet?

U va - rot, va - rot, va - rot, Da va - rot ba - tyush - ki - nikh.
At the __ gate, the gate, the gate, the gar - den gate shall we __ meet?

65
legato
Ai, Du - naii moy Du naii, Ai, ve - syo - lyi Du - naii.
Ah, Du - naii, my Du - naii, Ah, dear - est dear Du - naii.
legato
Ah, Ah,
legato
Ah, Ah,
legato
Ah, Ah,
69
p
Oo
p
Oo
mf (leggiero)
Ra - zü - gra - lí - sya ria - bya - ta, Ras - po - te shi - lis.
If we see the child - ren play - ing, They won't hear me say - ing.
(mp)

div.
rall.
mf
Ai, Du - naii moy Du - naii, Ai, ve - syo -
Ah, Du - naii my Du - naii, Ah, dear - est
Ai, Du - naii moy Du - naii, Ai,
Ah, Du - naii my Du - naii, Ah,
76
a tempo
lyi Du - naii.
dear Du - naii.
Du - naii.
mp

La Cucaracha
(The Cockroach)

from Mexico

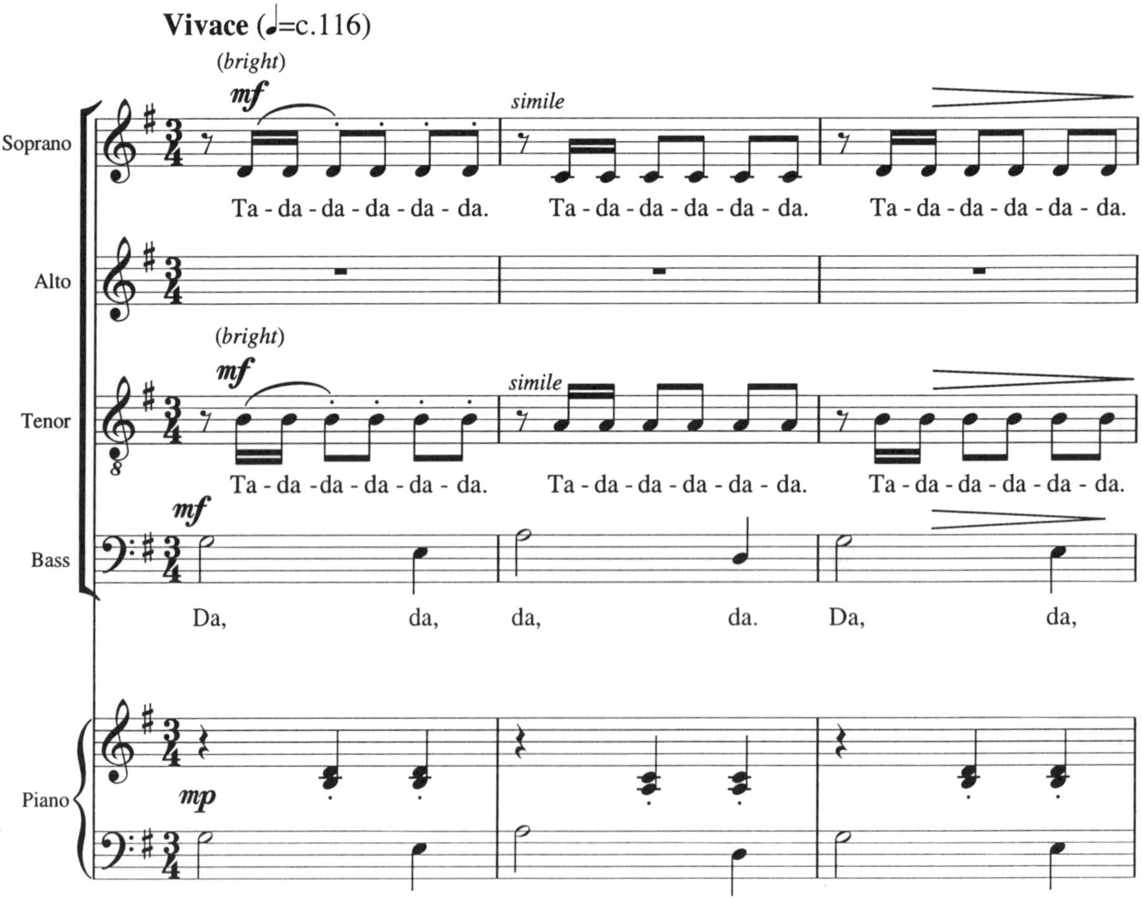

4
mp
Ta - da - da - da - da - da. Ta - da - da - da - da - da. Ta - da - da - da - da - da.
mf
To - das las mu - cha - chas tie - ren
mp
Ta - da - da - da - da - da. Ta - da - da - da - da - da. Ta - da - da - da - da - da.
mp
da, da. Da, da, da, da.
7
Ta - da - da - da - da - da. Ta - da - da - da - da - da. Ta - da - da - da - da - da.
en los o - jos dos es - tre - llas pe - ro las me - xi - ca -
Ta - da - da - da - da - da. Ta - da - da - da - da - da. Ta - da - da - da - da - da.
Da, da, da, da. Da, da,

10
f
Ta - da - da - da - da - da. Ta - da - da - da - da - da, ta - da - da. La cu - ca-
ni - tas de se - gu - ro son más be - llas. La cu - ca-
Ta - da - da - da - da - da. Ta - da - da - da - da - da, ta - da - da. La cu - ca-
da, da. Da, da, da, da, da. La cu - ca-
13
ra - cha, la cu - ca - ra - cha, Ya no quie - re ca - mi - nar. Por - qué no
ra - cha, la cu - ca - ra - cha, Ya no quie - re ca - mi - nar. Por - qué no
ra - cha, la cu - ca - ra - cha, Ya no quie - re ca - mi - nar. Por - qué no
ra - cha, la cu - ca - ra - cha, Ya no quie - re ca - mi - nar. Por - qué no

17
tie - ne, por - qué le fal - ta di - ne - ro pa - ra gas -
tie - ne, por - qué le fal - ta di - ne - ro pa - ra gas -
tie - ne, por - qué le fal - ta di - ne - ro pa - ra gas -
tie - ne, por - qué le fal - ta di - ne - ro pa - ra gas -
20
mf
simile
tar. Ta - da - da - da - da - da. Ta - da - da - da - da - da. Ta - da - da - da - da - da-
mf
simile
tar. Ta - da - da - da - da - da. Ta - da - da - da - da - da. Ta - da - da - da - da - da-
tar.
tar. Da, da.
mp

23
mp
tar. Ta - da da - da - da - da. Ta - da da - da - da - da. Ta - da da - da - da - da.
mp
tar. Ta - da da - da - da - da. Ta - da da - da - da - da. Ta - da da - da - da - da.
mf
Las mu - cha - chas son de o - ro, las ca - sa - das son de
mp
Da, da, da, da. Da, da,
mp
26
Ta - da da - da - da - da. Ta - da da - da - da - da. Ta - da da - da - da - da.
Ta - da da - da - da - da. Ta - da da - da - da - da. Ta - da da - da - da - da.
pla - ta, y las viu - das son de co - bre,
da, da. Da, da, da, da.

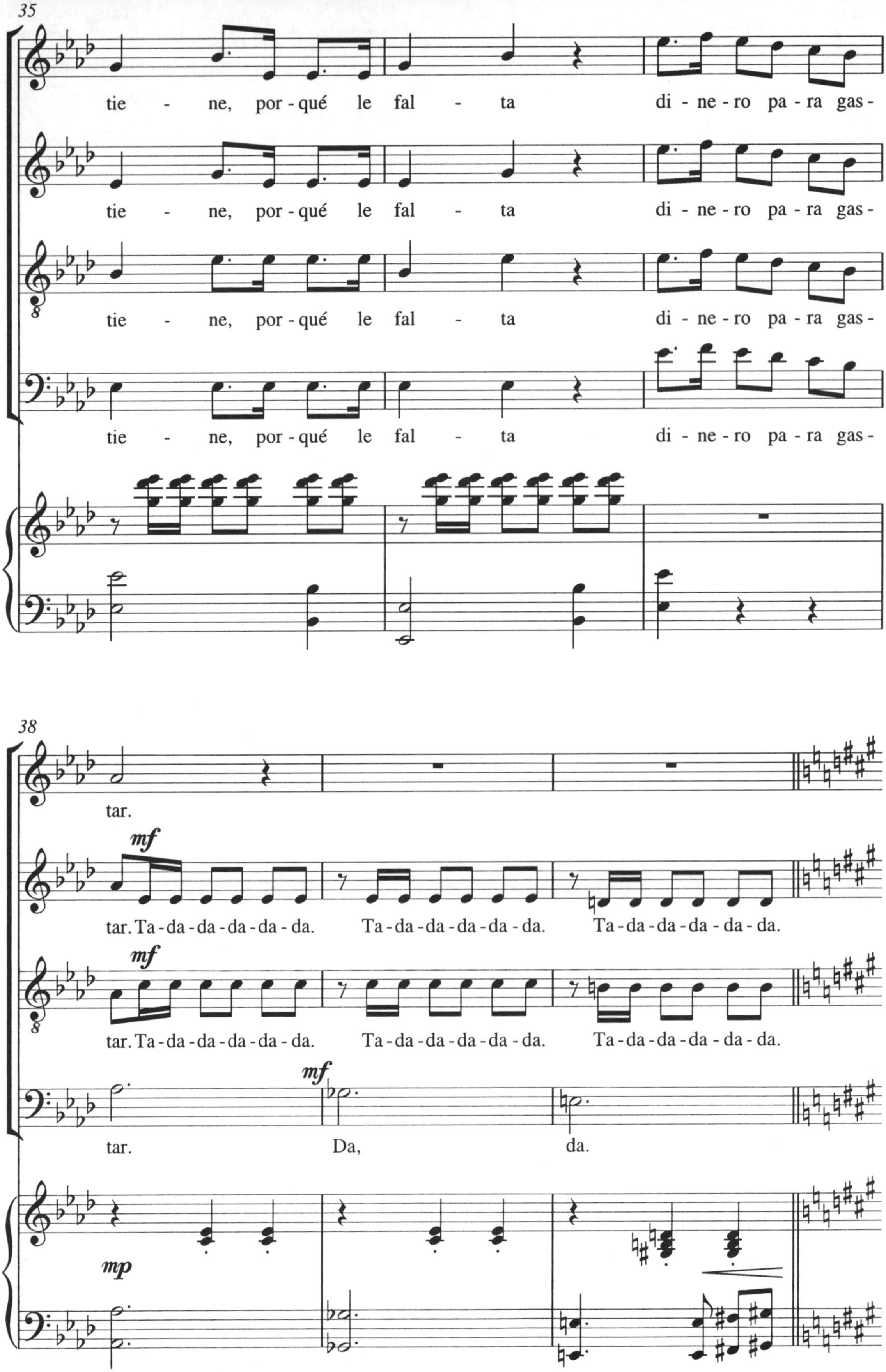

41
mf
U - na co - sa me da ri - sa. Pan - cho Vil - la sin ca-
mp
Ta - da - da - da - da - da. Ta - da - da - da - da - da. Ta - da - da - da - da - da.
mp
Ta - da - da - da - da - da. Ta - da - da - da - da - da. Ta - da - da - da - da - da.
mp
Da, da, da, da. Da, da,
mp
44
mi - sa. Ya se van los Car - ran - cis - tas,
Ta - da - da - da - da - da. Ta - da - da - da - da - da. Ta - da - da - da - da - da.
Ta - da - da - da - da - da. Ta - da - da - da - da - da. Ta - da - da - da - da - da.
da, da. Da, da, da, da.

por - qué vie - nen los Vill - is - tas. La cu - ca - ra - cha, la cu - ca-

Ta - da - da - da - da - da. Ta - da - da. La cu - ca - ra - cha, la cu - ca-

Ta - da - da - da - da - da. Ta - da - da. La cu - ca - ra - cha, la cu - ca-

Da, da, da, da, da. La cu - ca - ra - cha, la cu - ca-

ra - cha, Ya no quie - re ca - mi - nar. Por - qué no

ra - cha, Ya no quie - re ca - mi - nar. Por - qué no

ra - cha, Ya no quie - re ca - mi - nar. Por - qué no

ra - cha, Ya no quie - re ca - mi - nar. Por - qué no

24

53
tie - ne, por - qué le fal - ta di - ne - ro pa - ra gas -
tie - ne, por - qué le fal - ta di - ne - ro pa - ra gas -
tie - ne, por - qué le fal - ta di - ne - ro pa - ra gas -
tie - ne, por - qué le fal - ta di - ne - ro pa - ra gas -
56
f
div.
tar. Ta - da - da - da - da - da. Ta - da - da - da - da - da. Ta - da - da - da - da - da.
f
tar. Ta - da - da - da - da - da. Ta - da - da - da - da - da. Ta - da - da - da - da - da.
ff
tar. La cu - ca - ra - cha, la cu - ca - ra - cha,
ff
tar. La cu - ca - ra - cha, la cu - ca - ra - cha,
ff

59

Ta-da-da-da-da-da. Ta-da-da-da-da-da. Ta-da-da-da-da-da.

Ta-da-da-da-da-da. Ta-da-da-da-da-da. Ta-da-da-da-da-da.

Ya no quie-re ca-mi-nar, Por-qué no tie - ne, por-qué le

Ya no quie-re ca-mi-nar, Por-qué no tie - ne, por-qué le

62

ff unis.

Ta - da - da - da - da - da. di - ne - ro pa - ra gas - tar. ¡O - lé!

ff

Ta - da - da - da - da - da. di - ne - ro pa - ra gas - tar. ¡O - lé!

fal - ta, di - ne - ro pa - ra gas - tar. ¡O - lé!

fal - ta, di - ne - ro pa - ra gas - tar. ¡O - lé!

(shout)

Lomir Sich Iberbetn
(Let Us Be Lovers Again)

Yiddish

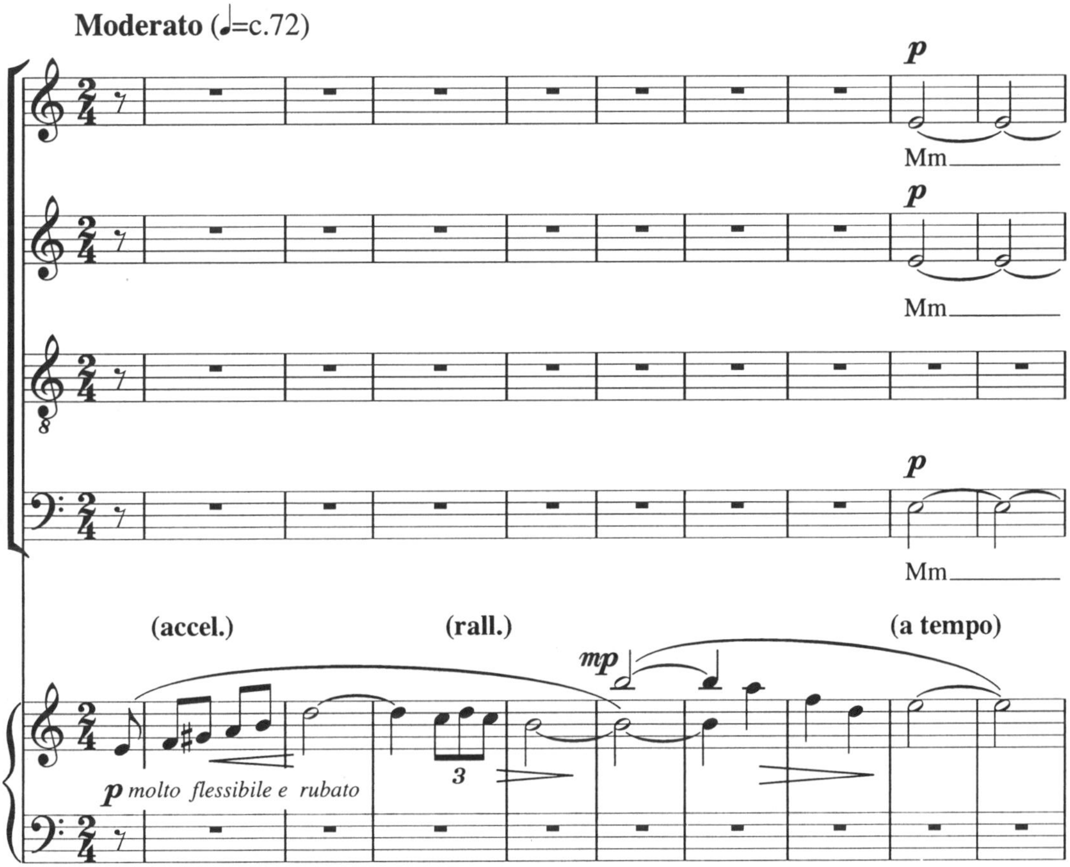

Lo - mir sich i - ber - be - tn, i - ber - be - tn, Hob af mir rach - mo - nes; Hob af mir rach-

mo - nes; Lo - mir sich i - ber - be - tn, C'h'ob dir lib sa - ko - nes, Lo - mir sich

22
i - ber - be - tn, C'h'ob dir lib sa - ko - nes.
mp
3
28
Più mosso (♩=c.84)
mp
Lo - mir sich i - ber - be - tn, i - ber - be - tn, Vos shtei - stu far der
Lo - mir, lo - mir, lo - mir, lo - mir,
Lo - mir, lo - mir, lo - mir, lo - mir,
Lo - mir, lo - mir, lo - mir, lo - mir,
Più mosso (♩=c.84)
mp più ritmico
molto distinto
mp

tir? Vos shtei - stu far der tir?_____ Lo - mir sich i - ber - be - tn, Kum a - rein zu

lo - mir, lo - mir, lo - mir, lo - mir, lo - mir, lo - mir,

lo - mir, lo - mir, lo - mir, lo - mir, lo - mir, lo - mir,

lo - mir, lo - mir, lo - mir, lo - mir, lo - mir, lo - mir,

mir._____ Lo - mir sich i - ber - be - tn, Kum a - rein zu mir.

lo - mir, lo - mir, lo - mir, lo - mir, lo - mir.

lo - mir, lo - mir, lo - mir, lo - mir, lo - mir.

lo - mir, lo - mir, lo - mir, lo - mir, lo - mir.

Più vivo (♩=c.100)
46
mf
Lo- mir, lo- mir, lo- mir, lo - mir,
mf
Lo- mir, lo- mir, lo- mir, lo - mir,
mf
Lo - mir, lo - mir, lo - mir, lo - mir,
mf
Lo - mir sich i - ber-be - tn, i - ber-be - tn, Loz di ma - men
Più vivo (♩=c.100)
accel.
mf
52
lo- mir, lo- mir, lo- mir, lo- mir, lo- mir, lo - mir,
lo- mir, lo- mir, lo- mir, lo- mir, lo- mir, lo - mir,
lo - mir, lo - mir, lo - mir, lo - mir, lo - mir, lo - mir,
vis - sn; Loz di ma - men vis - sn; Lo - mir sich i - ber - be - tn, Fùn li - be ge-

58
lo - mir, lo - mir lo - mir, lo - mir, lo - mir.
lo - mir, lo - mir, lo - mir, lo - mir, lo - mir.
- lo - mir, lo - mir, lo - mir, lo - mir, lo - mir.
-nis - sn, Lo - mir sich i - ber - be - tn, Fùn li - be ge - nis - sn.
63
Più vivo (♩=c.112)
f
Lo - mir sich i - ber - be - tn,
f
Lo - mir sich i - ber - be - tn,
accel.
Più vivo (♩=c.112)
f

68
mf
Kum a-rein zu mir.
i - ber - be - tn Vos shtei-stu far der tir? Vos shtei - stu far der
i - ber - be - tn Vos shtei-stu far der tir? Vos shtei - stu far der
mf
Kum a - rein zu
sim.
72
mf
Kum a-rein zu mir.
tir? Lo - mir sich i - ber - be - tn, Kum a - rein zu
tir? Lo - mir sich i - ber - be - tn, Kum a - rein zu
mir. Kum a - rein zu

Kum a - rein zu mir.   Kum a - rein zu mir.

mir.___ Lo - mir sich i - ber - be - tn, Kum a - rein zu mir.

mir.___ Lo - mir sich i - ber - be - tn, Kum a - rein zu mir.

mir.   Kum a - rein zu mir.

Più vivo (♩=c.130)

ff

Lo - mir sich i - ber - be - tn, i - ber - be - tn, Hob af mir rach - mo - nes;

Lo - mir sich i - ber - be - tn, i - ber - be - tn, Hob af mir rach - mo - nes;

Lo - mir sich i - ber - be - tn, i - ber - be - tn, Hob af mir rach - mo - nes;

Lo - mir sich i - ber - be - tn, i - ber - be - tn, Hob af mir rach - mo - nes;

Più vivo (♩=c.130)

ff

86

Hob af mir rach - mo - nes; Lo - mir sich i - ber - be - tn, C'h'ob dir lib sa -

91

ko - nes, Lo - mir sich i - ber - be - tn, C'h'ob dir lib sa - ko - nes.

Manthi'ki
(Spirit Song)

from Zimbabwe

Steady (♩=120), but with spirit

Nya - m'nje - nje w'e - nda ku - mba kwa - ke. We ye wo ye.

Nya - m'nje - nje w'e - nda ku - mba kwa - ke. We ye wo ye.

Nya - m'nje - nje w'e - nda ku - mba kwa - ke. We ye wo ye.

Nya - m'nje - nje w'e - nda ku - mba kwa - ke. We ye wo ye.

13
mf
Nya - m'nje - nje w'e - nda ku - mba kwa - ke. We ye wo ye.
mf
Nya - m'nje - nje w'e - nda ku - mba kwa - ke. We ye wo ye.
Tenor
mf
Nya - m'nje - nje w'e - nda ku - mba kwa - ke. We ye wo ye.
mf
17
(opt. descant)
f
Nya - m'nje - nje w'e - nda ku - mba kwa - ke. We ye wo ye.
f
Nya - m'nje - nje w'e - nda ku - mba kwa - ke. We ye wo ye.
f
Nya - m'nje - nje w'e - nda ku - mba kwa - ke. We ye wo ye.
f
Nya - m'nje - nje w'e - nda ku - mba kwa - ke. We ye wo ye.
f
Nya - m'nje - nje w'e - nda ku - mba kwa - ke. We ye wo ye.
f

21
mf
Shi - li - ma - ji - we ma - ji
mf
Shi - li - ma - ji - we ma - ji
Shi - li - ma - ji - we ma - ji
mf
Shi - li - ma - ji - we ma - ji
Shi - li - ma - ji - we ma - ji
mf
24
Shi - li - ma - ji - we ma - ji
mp
Shi - li - ma - ji - we ma - ji
mf
Shi - li - ma - ji - we ma - ji
mp
Shi - li - ma - ji - we ma - ji
mp
Shi - li - ma - ji - we ma - ji
mp

27
mf
Shi-li-ma - ji-we ma - ji
Shi-li-ma - ji-we ma - ji
Shi-li-ma - ji-we ma - ji
Nya - m'nje - nje
Shi-li-ma - ji-we ma - ji
Nya - m'nje - nje
30
Nya - m'nje - nje
w'e - nda ku - mba kwa - ke. We ye wo ye. Nya - m'nje - nje
w'e - nda ku - mba kwa - ke. We ye wo ye. Nya - m'nje - nje

41
mp
Shi - li - ma - ji - we ma - ji Shi - li - ma - ji - we ma - ji
mp
Shi - li - ma - ji - we ma - ji Shi - li - ma - ji - we ma - ji
Shi - li - ma - ji - we ma - ji
Shi - li - ma - ji - we ma - ji
mp
43
Shi - li - ma - ji - we ma - ji Shi - li - ma - ji - we ma - ji
Shi - li - ma - ji - we ma - ji Shi - li - ma - ji - we ma - ji
Shi - li - ma - ji - we ma - ji Shi - li - ma - ji - we ma - ji
Shi - li - ma - ji - we ma - ji Shi - li - ma - ji - we ma - ji

45
S1 only
mp
Shi - li mb'lu - ka, mb'lu - ka, shi - li mb'lu - ka, mb'lu - ka, shi - li
mp
shi - li
mp
Shi - li mb'lu - ka, mb'lu - ka, shi - li
mp
48
S1
S2
mf
mb'lu - ka, mb'lu - la, shi - li mb'lu - ka, mb'lu - ka, shi - li
mf
mb'lu - ka, mb'lu - ka, shi - li mb'lu - ka, mb'lu - ka, shi - li
mf
mb'lu - ka, mb'lu - ka, shi - li mb'lu - ka, mb'lu - ka, shi - li
mf
shi - li
mf

mb'lu - ka, mb'lu - ka, shi - li mb'lu - ka, mb'lu - ka, shi - li

mb'lu - ka, mb'lu - ka, shi - li mb'lu - ka, mb'lu - ka, shi - li

mb'lu - ka, mb'lu - ka, shi - li mb'lu - ka, mb'lu - ka, shi - li

mb'lu - ka, mb'lu - ka, shi - li mb'lu - ka, mb'lu - ka, shi - li

mb'lu - ka, mb'lu - ka, shi - li mb'lu - ka, mb'lu - ka,

mb'lu - ka, mb'lu - ka, shi - li mb'lu - ka, mb'lu - ka,

mb'lu - ka, mb'lu - ka, shi - li mb'lu - ka, mb'lu - ka,

mb'lu - ka, mb'lu - ka, shi - li mb'lu - ka, mb'lu - ka,

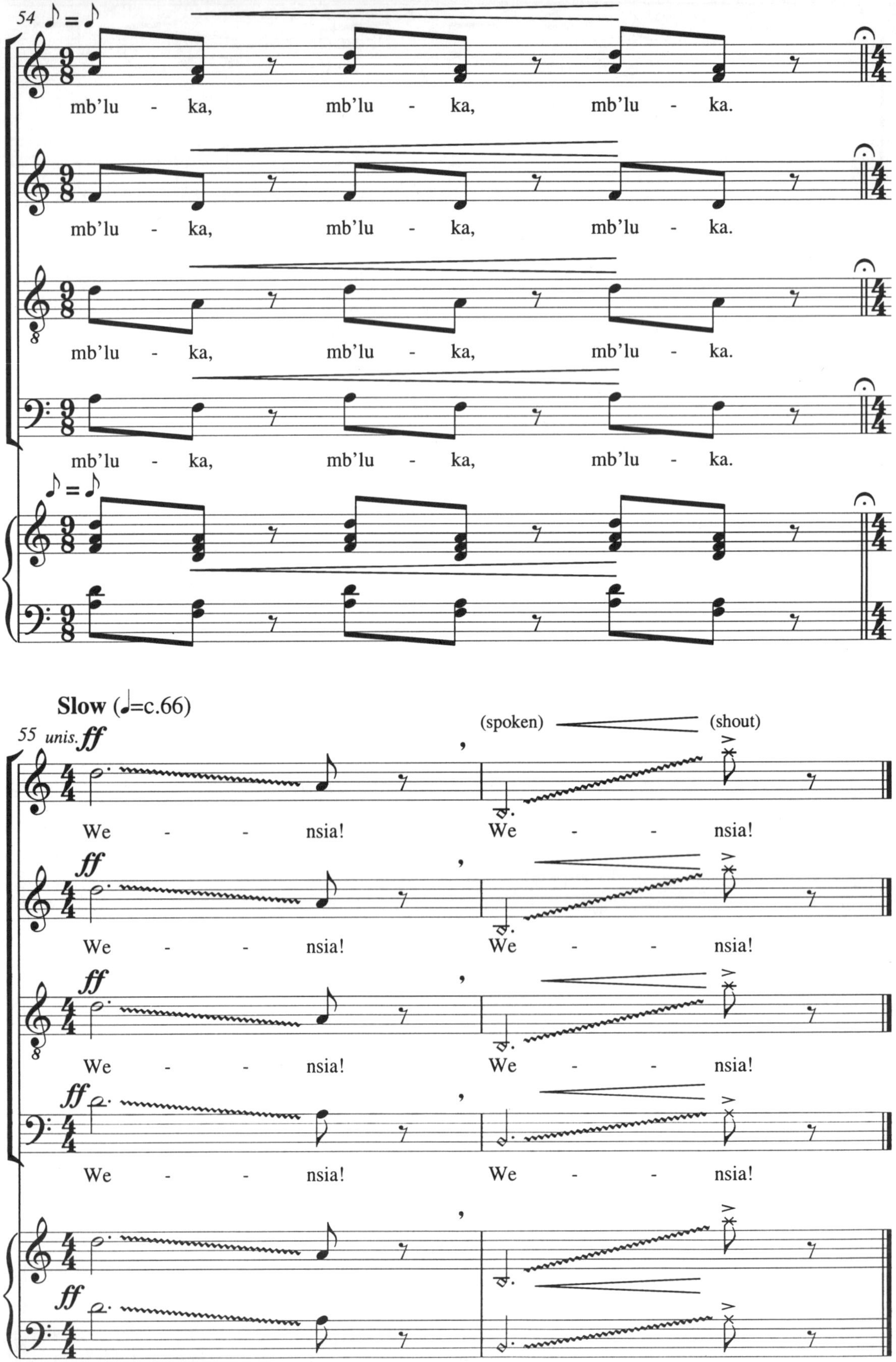
54
mb'lu - ka, mb'lu - ka, mb'lu - ka.
mb'lu - ka, mb'lu - ka, mb'lu - ka.
mb'lu - ka, mb'lu - ka, mb'lu - ka.
mb'lu - ka, mb'lu - ka, mb'lu - ka.
Slow (♩=c.66)
55 unis. ff
(spoken)
(shout)
We - - nsia! We - - nsia!
We - - nsia! We - - nsia!
We - - nsia! We - - nsia!
We - - nsia! We - - nsia!

Pescator Dell'Onda
(Fisherman From The Waves)

from Italy

Moderato scherzando (♩=72)

Piano

mf

Soprano *mf* ①

O pes-ca-tor dell'-on — da, O Fé-dé-ri! O

②

③

pes-ca-tor dell'-on — da, O Fé-dé-ri!

Tutti

Vie - ni pes-car in

12
quà, Col - la tu - a bel - la bar - ca, La tua bel - la se ne va. Fé - dé - ri, lin,
16
div.
la! Vie - ni pes - car in quà, Col - la tu - a bel - la bar - ca, La tua bel - la se ne
20
unis. p
va. Fè - dé - ri, lin, la! Vie -
Alto
mf
Vie - ni à pes - car mio an-

ni à pes-car mio an - nel - lo,__ O Fé-dé - ri! O Fé - dé -

- nel - lo, O Fé-dé - ri! Vie - ni à pes-car mio an-nel - lo, O Fé-dé-

mp

- ri!

ri! Che mi è ca - du - to in mar, Col - la tu - a bel - la

mf *8va*

mp

Che

bar-ca, La tua bel-la se ne va. Fé - dé - ri, lin, la! Che

8va *mf*

mi è ca-du-to in mar, Col-la tu-a bel-la bar-ca, La tua bel-la se ne va. Fé-dé-

mi è ca-du-to in mar, Col-la tu-a bel-la bar-ca, La tua bel-la se ne va. Fé-dé-

ri, lin, la!

ri, lin, la!

Tenor

L'an-nel-lo è già pes-ca - to, O Fé-dé-

ri! L'an-nel-lo è già pes-ca - to, O Fé-dé-ri! Cosa mi vo don - ar? Col - la tu - a bel - la bar - ca, La tua bel - la se ne va. Fé - dé -

ri, lin, la! Co - sa mi vo do - nar? Col - la tu - a bel - la

Bass
Co - sa mi vo do - nar? Col - la tu - a bel - la

Soprano
Ti

bar - ca, La tua bel - la se ne va. Fé - dé - ri, lin, la!

bar - ca, La tua bel - la se ne va. Fé - dé - ri, lin, la!

da - ró cen - to scu - di, O Fé-dé - ri! Ti da - ró cen - to scu - di, O Fé-dé

mp Oo, _____ Oo, _____ *div.*

mp Oo, _____ Oo, _____

mp Oo, _____ Oo, _____

ri! Sta bor - sa ri - ca - ma. Col - la tu - a bel - la

unis. mon - ey, mon-ey, mon - ey. Ah! _____ La, la, la, la,

Ah! _____ Ah! _____

Ah! _____

* Bars 59 - 68 are best unaccompanied, but the piano could support the voices if required.

barca, La tua bel-la se ne va, Fé-dé-ri, lin, la!

la, la, la, la, la, la, Fé-dé-ri, lin, la!

Fé-dé-ri, lin, la!

Fé-dé-ri, lin, la! Non

vo-le cen-to scu - di, O Fé-dé-ri! Non vo-le cen-to

mf legato

75
mp
Who wants to be a mil - lion - aire?
mf
Ne bor - sa a ri - ca -
scu - di, O Fé - dé - ri! Ne bor - sa a ri - ca - mar. Col - la tu - a bel - la

79
f
mar. La tua bel - la se ne va, Fé - dé - ri, lin,
bar - ca, La tua bel - la se ne va, Fé - dé - ri, lin,

82
f
la, la, la, la, la, la, la, la, la, la, la, la, la, la, la, la,
f
la, la, la, la, la, la, la, la, la, la, la, la, la, la, la, la,
ff
la! Vo - le un ba - cin d'a -
ff
la! Vo - le un ba - cin d'a -
84
la, la, la, la, la, la, la, la, la, la, la, la, la. doo - de -
la, la, la, la, la, la, la, la, la, la, la, la, la. doo - de -
mo - - re il tuo Fé - dé - ri! Vo -
mo - - re il tuo Fé - dé - ri! Vo -
3
LH
RH

86
doo doo - de - doo - de - doo - de - doo, doo, doo - de -
doo doo - de - doo - de - doo - de - doo, doo, doo - de -
le un ba - cin d'a - mo - re il tuo Fé - dé -
le un ba - cin d'a - mo - re il tuo Fé - dé -
88
doo doo - de - doo - de - doo - de - doo. Col - la tu - a bel - la
doo doo - de - doo - de - doo - de - doo. Col - la tu - a bel - la
ri! Che quel - lo pa - ghe - rá. Col - la tu - a bel - la
ri! Che quel - lo pa - ghe - rá. Col - la tu - a bel - la
LH
RH

91
bar - ca, La più bel - la se ne va, Fé - dé - ri, lin,
bar - ca, La più bel - la se ne va, Fé - dé - ri, lin,
bar - ca, La più bel - la se ne va, Fé - dé - ri, lin,
bar - ca, La più bel - la se ne va, Fé - dé - ri, lin,
94
la! Che quel - lo pa - ghe - rá. Col - la tu - a bel - la
la! Che quel - lo pa - ghe - rá. Col - la tu - a bel - la
la! Che quel - lo pa - ghe - rá. Col - la tu - a bel - la
la! Che quel - lo pa - ghe - rá. Col - la tu - a bel - la
LH
RH

97
bar - ca, La più bel - la se ne va. Fé - dé - ri,
bar - ca, La più bel - la se ne va. Fé - dé - ri,
bar - ca, La più bel - la se ne va. Fé - dé - ri,
bar - ca, La più bel - la se ne va. Fé - dé - ri,
100
lin, la!
lin, la!
lin, la!
lin, la!
9197